GOOD · OLD · DAYS

Live It Again™

1944

To Have and to Hold!

WAR BONDS

Contents

On the Home Front

With the establishment of the draft for World War II, the nation was quickly drained of manpower. Soldiers at first stayed on US soil, but with the invasion of Europe in the summer of 1944, that all changed. Women began to fill in the work roles of men in industry, and children took over many responsibilities around the home.

At first there was reluctance to draft fathers, but as the need for manpower increased, that slowly changed. Another unpopular move by the military was the drafting of 18-year-olds.

In many cases, there were major population shifts as women and children followed their husbands to bases on the west coast and in other parts of the country. Many people left the rural areas and headed for cities. Housing was increasingly difficult to find in industrial centers.

Due to gas rationing, transportation patterns changed as people carpooled or took public transportation, which was seriously overcrowded. Very few people took vacations, due to rationing, but also because trains were overbooked.

Fathers would seize every opportunity that they could to spend time with their children before being transferred overseas.

Children were taught to respect and look up to those in the military as role models of national allegiance and dedication.

Social times were few and far between, but when they did occur, they provided a boost to military morale.

Everyday Life

Around town

The phrase "mother's little helpers" became true in a hurry when fathers and older brothers were drafted for military service. "Chores" was a common word for those left at home. Children were asked to take care of animals, carry in wood for burning and assist with helping mother carry everything from buckets of water to groceries.

Many of those men left behind became neighborhood handymen, assisting with repairs and house maintenance needs for families where men were away at war. In most towns, neighbors looked after each other like one large family. Firemen, streetcar workers, zoo workers, school teachers and other public figures became friends with children whose father was overseas.

Most families didn't have much money to spend beyond their needs, but corner ice cream stores, candy shops and cheap movies gave options for times when children were given a special outing. Most treats, however, were a result of homemade baking.

Community helpers became friends with children, providing role models and listening ears to those whose fathers were gone.

Children were all called upon to help with family chores, such as carrying groceries to the car from the grocery store.

A bicycle ride or walk with close friends provided a good break to relax and reflect in the midst of tough times.

Neighbors served as helpers and repairmen for families whose men had gone to war.

Everyday Life

Around the Neighborhood

Women learned to work together to assist each other with outside work that normally would be done by the men.

The mailman was a welcome guest, especially when he brought letters from husbands and fathers overseas.

© 1944 SEP

THE SATURDAY EVENING

POST

MAY 13, 1944   10¢

What Really Happened at Teheran
By FORREST DAVIS

Beginning
Devil on His Trail
By JOHN and WARD HAWKINS

REPRINTED WITH PERMISSION OF AGFA ANSCO

Neighbors always had time for a visit with those around them, in many cases sharing news about loved ones.

The Metro Daily News

FINAL EDITION

JANUARY 5, 1944

THE DAILY MAIL CROSSES THE OCEAN

It becomes the first transoceanic newspaper.

© 1944 SEPS

"Sooner or later some girl shows up!"

On the Home Front

Romance military style

The role of the military in romance not only inspired service personnel and provided enjoyable times for our nation's ladies that looked up to them. The destinies of many families were also influenced by the crossing of paths that wouldn't have occurred without military commission.

Many romances began near bases when soldiers would go into town for social activities during time off. Sometimes letter correspondence would begin that would carry through a complete tour of duty, and then blossom upon return. At military canteens, women would provide food, books, magazines and homemade items to support the troops.

In communities close to military bases, many local girls found their ways to dances and parties in search of the soldier of their dreams. Such would often be considered a prize catch among the ladies of the community.

Whitman's chocolates from a favorite soldier was a special way to say "I love you."

REPRINTED WITH PERMISSION FROM RUSSELL STOVER CANDIES

A box of goodies and special gifts from a soldier were deeply appreciated during the more lonely hours.

Hitting the dance floor was a popular way for soldiers to socialize and take a break from the rigors of the military.

"Better say something nice about the propellers—she makes 'em."

Bands provided lively music for servicemen to enjoy at canteen-sponsored dances. This band performed at the St. Patrick's Day dance sponsored by the Washington Labor Canteen.

Dancing was a popular activity at canteens, and this twirling couple certainly enjoyed it. But others with two left feet (or just tired feet) could still enjoy themselves by watching all of the activity or chatting with friends.

Rest & Relaxation

A night out

Canteens provided servicemen with free refreshments and entertainment. Live bands, dancing, food and hot coffee took soldiers' minds off of the war while uplifting their spirits. All servicemen were welcomed at the canteen. Men and women mingled freely with servicemen from other Allied nations and even celebrities. One never knew who might drop in unexpectedly, especially at canteens in New York and Hollywood. On one Christmas Eve, Bing Crosby and his family sang Christmas carols to surprised servicemen at the Hollywood Canteen.

Separated from the bustling crowd on the dance floor, this sailor and a young woman found a quieter place to relax and talk.

With refreshments and entertainment, canteens were the place to be when young servicemen wanted to go out for a night on the town. These young women served soda pops and other refreshments to a crowd of thirsty servicemen.

Catching up on life over a soda or cup of coffee in the local café often placed the soldiers in a celebrity status when they returned home.

Soldiers returning to the family for a brief moment found household chores to be a pleasure while sharing special moments with loved ones.

PFC Charles Platt

"Look here, Huff, don't you ever have any fun on shore leave?"

Family moments singing, reading and embracing children passed all too quickly before soldiers were scheduled to leave for duty once again.

Rest & Relaxation

On leave

A "leave" for those in military could mean anything from a couple of days off base to a long enough reprieve to catch a few days with friends and relatives for a special holiday. Quite often, the holiday leave would occur for those still on bases in the United States.

Those overseas would take a few hours to play cards, attend a show, sometimes highlighting a touring United States celebrity, or they would visit sites of local significance.

Those fortunate enough to return home would spend time catching up with family members, looking at recent photographs and sharing their experiences with eager listeners.

A relic from some far-off country was greeted with amazement to those in local communities.

© 1944 SEPS

The Metro Daily News FINAL EDITION

JANUARY 15, 1944

EARTHQUAKE SHAKES SAN JUAN

The worst natural disaster in Argentina's history, it kills an estimated 10,000 people.

Rest & Relaxation

Washington Labor Canteen

The United Federal Workers of America opened the Washington Labor Canteen on Feb. 13, 1944 with much fanfare and excitement. The opening drew First Lady Eleanor Roosevelt, folk singer Peter Seeger and a crowd of servicemen and hostesses. Although it didn't draw as many celebrities as the canteens in New York and Hollywood, the Washington Labor Canteen was very popular among servicemen. Its dances gave soldiers and hostesses hours of amusement.

WIKIMEDIA PUBLIC DOMAIN PHOTOGRAPH

Folk musician Peter Seeger entertained the audience at the opening of the Washington Labor Canteen. Seated next to a young sailor, Eleanor Roosevelt listened as Seeger sang "When We March into Berlin."

© 1944 SEPS

JEFF KEATE

"Would you believe it if I told you you're the first girl I've dance with in over three years?"

The Washington Labor Canteen packed a crowd on its opening day. Eleanor Roosevelt arrived to show her support of the canteen and its service to America's heroes.

The Metro Daily News

FINAL EDITION

THE WEATHER

VOLUME 5 — No. 181

FEBRUARY 3, 1944

U.S. TROOPS CAPTURE MARSHALL ISLANDS

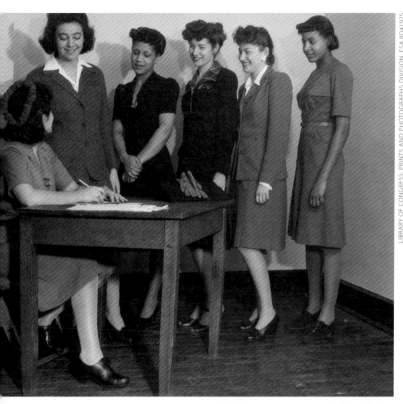

FAMOUS BIRTHDAYS

Alice Walker, February 9
American writer
Carl Bernstein, February 14
American journalist
Dennis Farina, February 29
American actor

Many women attended the dances and activities of the Washington Labor Canteen to uplift the spirits of the servicemen.

Eleanor Roosevelt and an audience of servicemen and hostesses listened to folk artist Carile Tart, of the District of Columbia recreation committee, sing folk songs at the opening of the Washington Labor Canteen.

Everyday Life

Fatherhood begins

For many fathers in World War II, information about their young child came in a letter from home thousands of miles away. Some children were born right after fathers had gone to war. At home, mothers would attempt to fill the role of both parents in attending ballgames, school functions and giving advice.

When letters from the service would arrive from the father, mothers would try to relay the life and love of their father. Anxious fathers would sometimes break with emotion or shout with enthusiasm when letters arrived giving the latest details and happenings of their children.

Once fathers finally did arrive home, many of them made every effort possible to make up for the experiences they had missed while they were gone. Sometimes, there was quite an adjustment to make in family dynamics.

Fathers quickly learned to bond with their children in some of the "non-glory" activities when they arrived home from serving in the war.

REPRINTED WITH PERMISSION FROM AVIVA

© 1944 SEPS

"And quit calling me Pop!"

© 1944 SEPS

"Good night! A full house!"

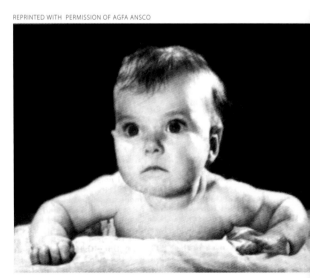

REPRINTED WITH PERMISSION OF AGFA ANSCO

so like you see that [kid?]. He weighs seven pounds and two ounces, which is, & course all is just right for a boy Of course all his eyes were blue at first but I think his are going to stay blue I hope so Anyway, don't you? Some pictures has

MRS MARY JONES
43 LAUREL LANE
GREENWICH CONN.

Pvt. JOE JONES 3764932
Co G 742 BON B.
APO B436
% POSTMASTER N.Y.C.

Everyday Life

Kids

Energy showed itself in many ways, including doing chin-ups on the swing set.

The family "pooch" was always good for a reassuring look, tail-wagging support or just plain friendship.

THE SATURDAY EVENING **POST**

MAY 20, 1944   10¢

How Soon Can We Knock Out Japan?
By ERNEST O. HAUSER

The Meanest Th
in the World
By MYRON M. STEARN

A sick sports fan eager to play with his friends looks through the window as boys run off to play baseball nearby.

Girls were often dressed in a fancy pinafore, complete with a matching ribbon in the hair.

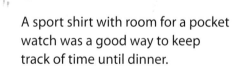

A sport shirt with room for a pocket watch was a good way to keep track of time until dinner.

Walking to and from school often gave good opportunity for a casual chat with a good friend.

Everyday Life

At the market

Goodies inside of glass cases were always an attraction to children as they counted out their money for a special treat at the local market. Occasionally, doing chores or a special deed for a neighbor would bring just enough change for a candy bar, licorice stick or scoop of ice cream.

Sometimes, trusting mothers would write a small list of groceries that were needed and send the children to purchase them. On other occasions, a visit to the market together would provide a special outing for family members.

The social aspect of meeting at the market, or hearing about things happening around the neighborhood also provided information to be taken home or to neighbors working in their yards.

Everyday life sometimes presented its challenges, such as discovering a flat tire in a parking zone just when hands are full of market purchases.

THE SATURDAY EVENING

POST

SEPTEMBER 23, 1944   10¢

BANKRUPT ITALY
IS CAPABLE OF ANYTHING
By ALLEN RAYMOND

WHAT THE
BUZZ BOMB MEANS TO YOU
MARTIN SOMMERS
DEMAREE BESS

FAMOUS BIRTHDAYS

Roger Daltrey, March 1 English musician of the band The Who
Diana Ross, March 26 American singer and member of The Supremes
Denny McLain, March 29 American baseball player

Sometimes it took a long time to decide about the purchase of a special treat, as is reflected on the face of the store owner here waiting for a young boy to make up his mind.

What Made Us Laugh

"Rafferty? I dunno, he was here a minute ago."

"Discouraging, isn't it?"

"Mr. Haddock! Mr. Smith! I've found Mr. Turnbull!"

"Which of you is the 'solid little female character' that 'cut a mean rug' at the USO dance last night?"

"Couldn't I be on the ground crew?"

"I'm unhappy here!"

"I warned you not to stay in there too long!"

"That's Mr. Kranz, the retired butcher."

The rationing office was always filled with citizens appealing certain needs or seeking to work through the problems of a very encumbered system.

"You mind explaining shoe rationing to them?"

"A story like that deserves a bigger audience! Have you considered putting it in a novel?"

Rationing

A daily challenge

Movies such a, *Rationing* and *Overview for Rationing*, the story of a small-time butcher who has trouble coping with meat rationing, reflected the experience the nation was going through in sacrificing for troops overseas.

Americans were asked to sacrifice usage of gasoline, meat, butter and many other everyday products to accommodate financial and product support for the war in the European and Pacific fronts.

In addition to the bureaucracy of it all, hardships were even heightened when rationing stamps would be lost or stolen. The loss of gas rationing stamps on short trips could cause a real predicament for people needing gas to return home.

During 1944, meat rationing was minimized for several months, and was reinstituted at the end of the year.

"OF COURSE I CAN!

I'm patriotic as can be —
And ration points won't worry me!"

The Metro Daily News

FINAL EDITION

MARCH 18, 1944

ITALY'S MOUNT VESUVIUS ERUPTS
Dozens are killed and thousands flee their homes.

FAMOUS BIRTHDAYS
Tony Orlando, April 3 American musician
John Milius, April 11 American film director, producer and screenwriter
Richard Kline, April 29 American actor and television director

DON'T LET GENERAL MacARTHUR DOWN— BUY WAR BONDS!

The Timken Roller Bearing Company, Canton, Ohio

War Bonds

Industry's efforts

Industrial leaders, realizing that war bonds were a strong source of financing for their business, found ways to promote their sales, such as advertising on the sides of trucks and on their products. The sale of bonds was a popular way to raise money for war product financing, and allowed for the opportunity to rally around their purchase as a patriotic duty. Industries and businesses sought to encourage their purchase by their own involvement in buying bonds, and then advertising those purchases to generate public enthusiasm.

War bonds financed production of the war industry, from small personal equipment to heavy machinery.

Buy an **EXTRA** WAR BOND

Advertising the sale of war bonds on the sides of trucks and on products was a popular way for industry to promote war bonds.

FAMOUS BIRTHDAYS

George Lucas, May 14 American film director and producer

John Newcombe, May 23 Australian tennis player

Gladys Knight, May 28 American singer and lead singer of Gladys Knight and the Pips

THE SATURDAY EVENING
POST
NOW WE CAN LICK TYPHUS
By ALLEN RAYMOND
The Collaborator
By JOHN W. THOMASON, JR.
Mead Schaeffer

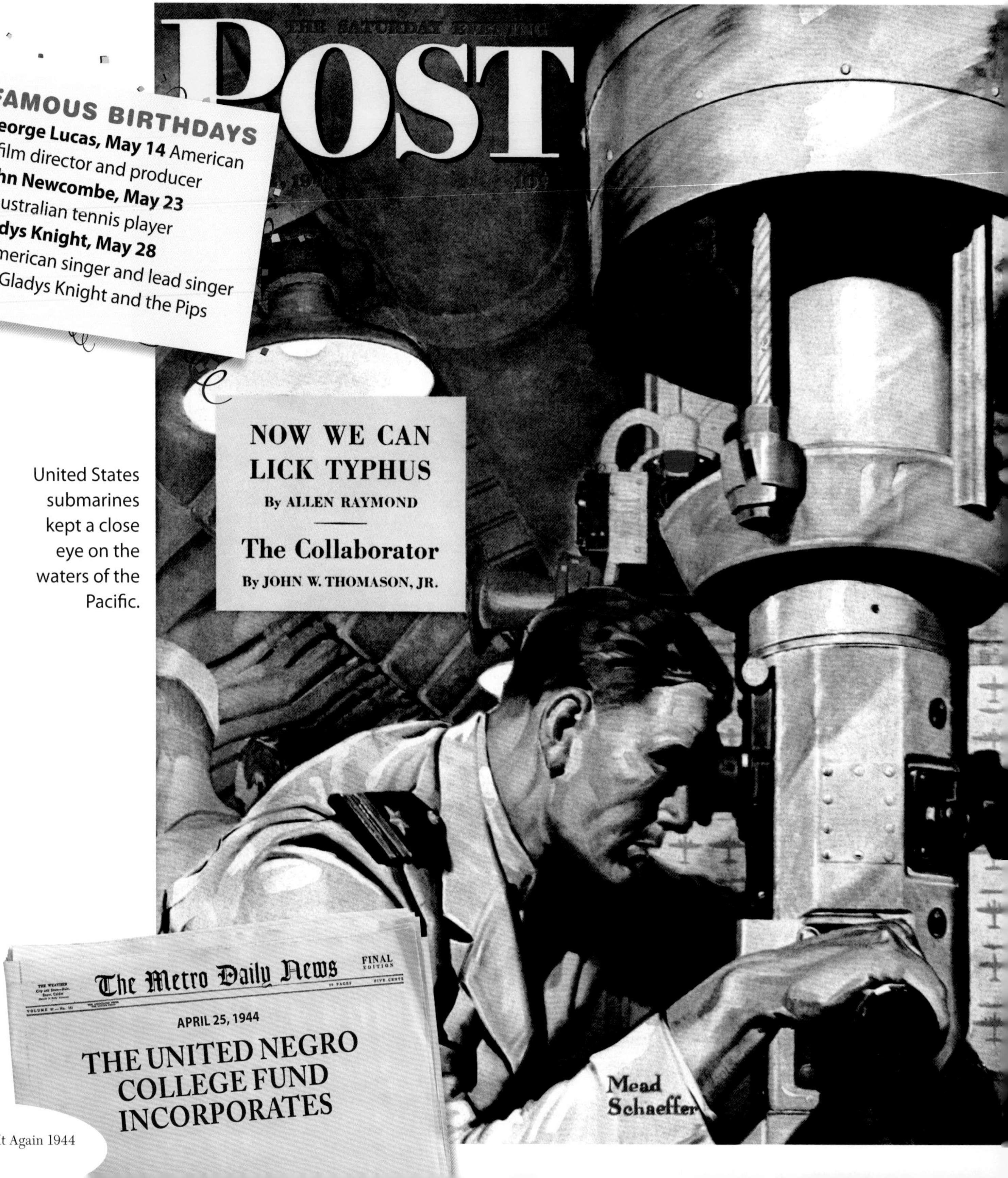

United States submarines kept a close eye on the waters of the Pacific.

The Metro Daily News

FINAL EDITION

APRIL 25, 1944

THE UNITED NEGRO COLLEGE FUND INCORPORATES

Military Action

Military action saw several climactic battles during 1944, beginning with the Allied victory on D-Day. From Normandy's shores, Allied forces went on the offensive, winning the Battle of Brittany, liberating Paris and capturing Aachen, the first German city to fall to the Allies. But the Germans continued to fight.

In mid-December, German forces began the Battle of the Bulge in Belgium's Ardennes Mountains region. Even though the German offensive surprised the Allies, they handed the Germans a stunning defeat.

In the Pacific Campaign, the Allies experienced a major success as well. Filipino and Allied forces defeated Japanese Imperial forces at the Battle of Leyte, the largest naval battle of World War II. By late December, the entire island was under Allied control.

Allied forces constructed Mulberry Harbor following the D-Day invasion as a place to offload everything they would need to sustain the offensive into the heart of German-occupied Europe.

U.S. tanks and infantry men trudged through deep snow during the Battle of the Bulge in December 1944.

Although Allied forces met little resistance as they swept through northern Brittany, German forces inflicted heavy casualties in port cities like Brest, where these American soldiers fought. The fighting left the city in ruins, and German forces surrendered Sept. 18, 1944.

Women in Uniform

Industry's efforts

With the men away at war, the opportunities for women to serve in the workplace and in the military exploded. The government's ad campaigns enticed women to enlist in the new military branches created for them. Businesses and industry ran ads encouraging women's service as well. The reasoning was simple: The more women who could fill non-combat jobs, the more men who could serve on the front lines, and the quicker the war could be won. With women entering what was once a man's world, many of the ads portrayed women as true ladies—classy, strong and beautiful.

Canada Dry Ginger Ale toasted the women of the United States Armed Forces in this advertisement.

It's a grand and glorious feeling

Enlist in the WAVES

INQUIRE AT ANY
Navy Recruiting Station or Office of Naval Officer Procurement

From medicine and intelligence to science, technology and communications, opportunities for women to serve in the military abounded.

YOUR DUTY ASHORE ... HIS AFLOAT

SPARS

APPLY NEAREST COAST GUARD OFFICE

Pitch in and Help!

JOIN THE WOMEN'S LAND ARMY OF THE U.S. CROP CORPS

More than 1 million women donned work clothes and headed out to the farms as part of the Women's Land Army of the U.S. Crop Corps. Women filled in where at one time only men could be seen harvesting crops, milking cows and driving tractors.

The Cadet Nurse Corps became the first
federal program to grant money for
education directly to students in addition
to funds given directly to schools.

Women in Uniform

Nurses needed

The magnitude of World War II opened an enormous need for nurses in the armed services. Prior to the war, there were 8,000 military nurses. That changed with the bombing of Pearl Harbor. As the war progressed, the numbers increased to 59,000 in the Army and 11,000 in the Navy. Such numbers helped fill the gap but did not eliminate it. A nurse shortage continued throughout the war, prompting advertising campaigns and the development of the Cadet Nurse Corps, a program promising young women a free education.

While nurses in Europe found themselves in field hospitals near the front lines, nurses in the Pacific Theater were stationed near enough to receive wounded soldiers by air yet far enough away to avoid an enemy ground threat.

At Red Cross Canteens, like this one, nurses mingled with servicemen and volunteers from the Red Cross Canteen Corps.

THE WEATHER
City and Entire State
Sunny, Cooler
Details in Story elsewhere

The Metro Daily News

FINAL EDITION

VOLUME IV — No. 101

20 PAGES   FIVE CENTS

MAY 5, 1944

GANDHI RELEASED FROM INDIAN PRISON

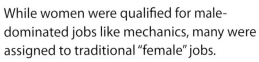

While women were qualified for male-dominated jobs like mechanics, many were assigned to traditional "female" jobs.

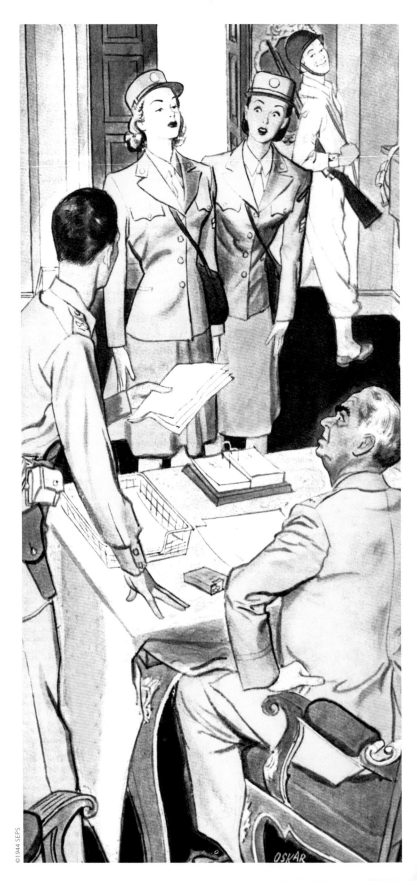

Women in Uniform

At work

Women's jobs during WWII were vast and varied. From the factories and shipyards to the military branches and the government, women entered the workforce in astounding numbers. Women filled crucial roles in scientific research and intelligence gathering, often handling highly classified information. On the ground in Europe, members of the Women's Army Corps (WACs) received, translated and decoded reports from the French Resistance and took over duties at abandoned German switchboards. Other women's scientific research helped usher in the nuclear age.

Many WACs served as administrative assistants to Army officers.

The media was intrigued by the idea of women serving in the military and published mostly favorable newspaper and magazine content.

"Yeah? Well, ad-da-da-da-da-da-da—da-da-dit-da-dit-da-dit-dit to you too!"

Around the Neighborhood

At your service

Door to door service was one of the ways businesses increased their customers. In many cases they were also accommodating families with need. With many fathers and husbands off to war, it was helpful to busy mothers to not have to go out of the house to acquire special purchases such as milk and bread.

For many children of the time, the moment that the milkman came was always an exciting moment, especially if Mom had ordered a special treat such as chocolate milk. The dropping of the milk box lid was a daily sound around the neighborhood as the concept of home-delivered milk quickly became an institution.

As was the case with oil men and mailmen, deliverers became neighborhood friends to all of their customers and sources of community tidbits of what was going on in the area. In some cases, milkmen even delivered "mail" as customers often used their services to deliver notes to neighbors down the street.

G.I.'s lockers around the world contained copies of this promotional photo of actress Betty Grable. The photo and a string of movies, including 1944's *Pin Up Girl*, made Grable the highest paid actress in America.

Starring Bing Crosby as Father Chuck O'Malley, *Going My Way* was the top grossing film of 1944. The story about a young catholic priest with a worldly past earned top honors at the Academy Awards. It captured Best Picture, Best Director, Best Actor and Best Supporting Actor awards.

The Big Screen

Hollywood's films in 1944 did more than just entertain. From happily-ever-after musicals and inspirational stories to tragic crime dramas, movies gave Americans an escape, built morale, educated the public and distributed information. Movies in 1944 also contributed to the emergence of a new style of filmmaking. American film noir was characterized by crime dramas, strange camera angles, dark shadows and hard lighting.

FAMOUS BIRTHDAYS
Jeffrey Tambor, July 8
American actor
Jan-Michael Vincent, July 15
American actor
Geraldine Chaplin, July 31
American actress/musician

Meet Me in St. Louis introduced "The Trolley Song," "The Boy Next Door," and "Have Yourself a Merry Little Christmas." Starring Judy Garland, the film was nominated for a string of Academy Awards. Although Garland initially rejected the role as too juvenile, she later considered the part of Esther Smith as one of her favorites.

© CORBIS

THE WEATHER
City and State—Rain,
Snow, Colder

The Metro Daily News

FINAL EDITION

VOLUME 97 — No. 161   20 PAGES   FIVE CENTS

JUNE 6, 1944

ON D-DAY EISENHOWER COMMANDS AS ALLIED TROOPS STORM NORMANDY, FRANCE BEACHES

Stars in War

Entertaining the troops

Bringing laughter, joy and a taste of home, pop culture's most famous entertainers traveled to every area of the world where U.S. servicemen could be found. The United Service Organization (USO) organized camp shows, giving stars the opportunity to lift servicemen's morale with a witty joke or a simple song. Big names like Bing Crosby, James Cagney, Fred Astair, Marlene Dietrich, Jack Benny, Bob Hope, Humphrey Bogart, Clark Gable, Walt Disney and Duke Ellington participated in USO camp shows in Europe, North Africa and the western Pacific. Stateside, stars entertained servicemen in canteens and through broadcasts on Armed Forces Radio Shows.

Jack Benny, seen here with Commander W.J. Wicks, traveled to Majuro Atoll in the Marshall Islands in September 1944 to perform at a camp show. A sign naming the building in the background "The Beautiful Post-War Majuro Biltmore" welcomed the comedian to the island.

Actress and singer Betty Hutton, caught tasting food in front of a crowd of amused sailors and Marines, performed for U.S. servicemen in the Marshall Islands.

Entertainers Frank Sinatra, Dinah Shore and Bing Crosby came together with Major Mann Holiner to record an Armed Forces Radio Show.

Bob Hope, shown here with his wife Dolores, logged more than 30,000 miles and performed more than 150 times as he traveled throughout the South Pacific in the summer of 1944.

"Would you give these notes to the 2nd, 4th, 5th, 6th, 8th and 10th from the left?"

With its rough terrain and heavy defenses, many strategists believed Omaha Beach was an unlikely location for a major invasion. Nevertheless, 50,000 American soldiers waded ashore.

The Metro Daily News FINAL EDITION

THE WEATHER
City and State—Rain.
Snow, Colder

VOLUME 87—No. 151

19 PAGES   FIVE CENTS

JULY 6, 1944

1ST LT. JACKIE ROBINSON ARRESTED

After Robinson refused to move to the back of a segregated U.S. Army bus, he is taken into custody, but is later acquitted.

D-Day

Across the sea

D-Day began for Allied paratroopers just after midnight on Tuesday, June 6, 1944. Five hours later, troops began the assault on the beaches of Normandy, France. Poor weather conditions and confusion initially hampered Allied efforts, but the troops refused to face defeat. They achieved Allied objectives and began to take ground from Hitler's Nazis.

The D-Day victory gave Allied forces a strong foothold on Europe's mainland and set the stage for the eventual end of the war. From Normandy's 50-mile stretch of coastline, Allies pushed into the heart of German-occupied Europe, liberating grateful citizens in each town along the way.

General Dwight Eisenhower gave orders to American paratroopers in England just prior to D-Day. Paratroopers faced a difficult night jump behind enemy lines.

Not long after D-Day, Allied ships brought supplies to troops, enabling them to push farther into German-occupied Europe.

D-Day
In New York

When news of D-Day reached the United States, Americans gathered to learn as much as possible about the events on the shores of Normandy. In New York, citizens spilled into the streets. A D-Day rally and parade were organized, and churches and synagogues opened their doors for special services.

Hungry for information, people gathered outside the Times building to watch the newsline, tuned into radio reports and read newspaper articles. The headline on a special edition of the New York Times read "Allied Armies Land in France in the Havre-Cherbourg Area; Great Invasion is Under Way."

A crowd gathers outside New York City's Times building to watch information about the D-Day invasion scroll across the newsline.

American flags waved proudly as New Yorkers gathered for a D-Day rally. Mayor Fiorello La Guardia addressed the large crowd in Madison Square.

Some New Yorkers marched while others looked on during the parade celebrating the Allied victory in France. The parade and rally in New York's Madison Square were organized quickly when news of the invasion reached the U.S.

D-Day
In New York

Men crowded closely to read news of the D-Day invasion from a newspaper posted outside a storefront in Times Square.

News of Allies' victory in France prompted churches and synagogues to quickly prepare special services to mark the historic day. Saint Vincent de Paul's Church in New York organized a noon mass, and Congregation Emunath Israel, a synagogue on New York's West 23rd Street, announced it would be open for 24 hours for special services.

The Metro Daily News
FINAL EDITION

JULY 20, 1944

HITLER SURVIVES CLAUS VON STAUFFENBERG'S ASSASSINATION ATTEMPT

Concerned about the war and hopeful for a victorious end, New Yorkers gathered in Times Square. They stared at the newsline on the Times building, which displayed information about the Allies' successful invasion of France.

What Made Us Laugh

"Say, they're going pretty far with this obstacle course, aren't they?"

"I think probably I'm a square peg, if that's any help."

"Friend, foe, or figment of my imagination?"

"You needn't have gone to all that trouble, son. She's happy enough just to have a date."

"Of course, our cruising speed is around 400 miles per hour, Dad, but occasionally when in a power dive we hit 700!"

"Oh, all right! Polly wants a cracker—Sir!"

"To Private Donohue from the Trick Dice Company— Private Donohue! Has anyone seen Private Donohue?"

A school teacher took her class outdoors to teach the children how to plant and care for vegetables in the school's Victory Garden on First Avenue in New York City.

On the Home Front

Victory Gardens

With the strain the war effort placed on the country's food supply, the U.S. government encouraged families to show their patriotism by supplementing rations with fresh vegetables grown in their own gardens. Americans stepped up to the task. In little time, they transformed backyards, vacant city lots and rooftops into Victory Gardens. Neighbors formed cooperatives to share produce, and magazines published stories on gardening and canning. Victory Gardens fed the public and boosted morale. They gave proud Americans yet another way to support the war effort.

Farm families and other Americans living in rural areas had been gardening for generations, but that was a way of life urban residents didn't know. Still, patriotic citizens, like these in New York City, rolled up their sleeves and dug into the soil to support the war effort.

"Caw."

Liberation of Paris

Since the invasion of Normandy in early June, French Resistance in Paris had been tracking the progress of the Allied forces as they inched closer to the city. By mid-August, they could wait no longer, and skirmishes with the Germans began to break out.

Allied forces arrived in support of the French Resistance, officially liberating the city on Aug. 25, 1944. Church bells rang as thousands of proud Parisians flooded the streets to welcome the soldiers.

Before the city's liberation, Hitler had ordered that Paris be destroyed before it was surrendered, but the German official in charge of Paris failed to carry out that order. As a result, the many sites that made Paris a city of romance and cultural significance remained intact and gave Parisians another reason to celebrate.

Allied forces organized a "Victory Day" military parade through the streets of Paris on Aug. 29, 1944, several days after the city's liberation. U.S. tanks rolled through the Arc de Triomphe, and the U.S. 28th Infantry Division marched proudly down the Champs Elysees in front of cheering French citizens.

French patriots welcomed Allied troops and showed support of the president of the Provisional Government of the French Republic, Charles de Gaulle. On the day Paris was liberated, de Gaulle addressed the French with a passionate speech, in which he proclaimed, "Paris! Outraged Paris! Broken Paris! Martyred Paris! But liberated Paris!"

Rows of American troops marched down Paris' Champs Elysees as crowds of French welcome their liberators. Celebrations began with the city's official liberation on Aug. 25, 1944 and continued until the city's "Victory Day" parade on Aug. 29, 1944.

Tools of War

Many of the tools used in World War II were recycled from World War I. As geographies and war situations changed, they were recycled and put into use. Some were changed into "ducks," which could be used in water or on land. Bulldozers were fashioned to construct airfields and roads for battle. The American ability to rebuild and improvise proved to be a great asset, giving industry at home time to manufacture and supply needed machinery.

This Corsair fighter plane was supplied through the efforts of Good Year.

The automotive industry helped recondition, and then supply Jeeps for field work.

The Metro Daily News

FINAL EDITION

AUGUST 1, 1944

THE WARSAW UPRISING BEGINS

THE SATURDAY EVENING

POST

OCTOBER 28, 1944 10¢

BLONDIE

152

Japan Digs in to Die
By MARK GAYN

—————

**Edgar Snow Reports
on Germany's
Worst Crime**

Mead
Schaeffer

© 1944 SEPS

KEEP AMERICA STRONG
BUY MORE WAR BONDS

Special shipping tools were fashioned to transport landing craft and material for tanks.

Tools of War

Many of the tools of World War II, especially at the beginning, were remnants left over from World War I, or worked-over combinations from former wars.

Older vehicles were adapted for use in Europe until American industry could catch up with the war needs.

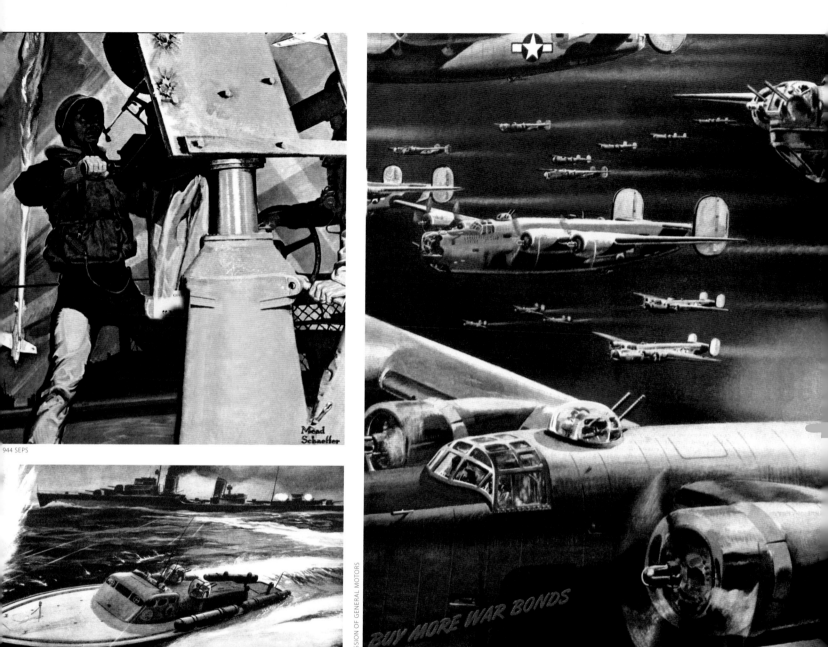

Mead
Schaeffer

BUY MORE WAR BONDS

...ctures of World War II machinery were often utilized to raise funding for war bonds to support the update of needed tools ...nd equipment.

Meltdown of steel and other types of metals originally used in the automotive industry became a necessity to recycle for war production.

On the Home Front

Industry at work

The huge demand of war vehicles, tools of war and all types of accompanying medical and mechanical needs to assist with the war effort forced a changeover in industrial products during the war years. Industries such as auto, airplane and other heavy-metal companies recycled their manufacturing materials to make weapons, machinery and vehicles for war usage. At first, jobs fell off, but once the changeover was complete, there was a dramatic increase in the work force to assist with war production.

Lifts were utilized to load American-produced products for shipment to war countries.

Trainloads of metal arrived at steel yards to be recycled for war usage.

Collection of scrap metal was the basis to meet manufacturing needs in making war materials.

On the Home Front

Women at work

During the war, women began to gain more respect as workforce potential. Men began to realize that women could work outside the home successfully and earn respectable incomes. While they filled many traditional female jobs, women also broke into jobs that had been held exclusively by men prior to the war, such as bank tellers, office management and sales people. Nearly one million women worked jobs in the federal government, often referred to as "government girls."

The ability to fill in for men while they were at war changed the entire image of women in the workforce. Most men were grateful their wives assisted with work outside the home while they were gone.

"When V-day comes, Alice isn't going to waste any time getting out of here!"

Women took on jobs traditionally held by men, such as farming, industrial skilled jobs and government employment.

Beach gear was still quite modest for most people, with one-piece bathing suits or beach robes part of the dress style.

An afternoon at the local pool often resulted in a time to make friends or relax with that special person in one's life.

For girls, getting together to trim each other's hair and doing each other's fingernails or makeup provided time to catch up on the latest "boy chatter."

© 1944 SEPS

The Metro Daily News

THE WEATHER
City and State—Rain, Snow, Colder

FINAL EDITION

28 PAGES   FIVE CENTS

VOLUME 27 — No. 181

SEPTEMBER 3, 1944

ALLIES LIBERATE BRUSSELS

Everyday Life

Summer Fun

Summer fun during 1944 was creative and simple, with little expense but lots of togetherness. Picnics at the local park, time on the beach and various inexpensive sports activities brought people together. Families would meet for Sunday dinners and play croquet, volleyball, softball and other outside activities.

Special getaways would often involve time at the closest beach or lake. Many communities had church softball leagues or youth baseball leagues. Gathering at the ball diamond with a bag of popcorn or homemade treats was a good way to catch up on what was going on around the neighborhood.

1944 SEPS

THE SATURDAY EVENING
POST
JULY 22, 1944   10¢

The Controversial Mr. Fly
By HENRY F. PRINGLE

"211 SURVIVORS ARRIVED TODAY"
By ALLEN RAYMOND

© 1944 SEPS

This illustration by Alex Ross shows one of the hobbies of the time. Both men and women enjoyed the challenge of the archery range.

Clothing was still modest, with even the most casual activities taking place in blouses for the ladies and jackets and hats for the men.

© 1944 SEPS

Everyday Life

On the water

Water recreation was a cheap way to have fun and even be a bit productive. Taking a fishing pole and bait to the local river or lake was commonplace for neighborhood fun. Boys enjoyed competing and bragging about catching the largest or most fish. Most families close to any body of water had a canoe or rowboat. Rowing was often a good way to communicate with that special friend or family members. Occasionally, rowers would forget themselves and end up much farther from home than they had planned. For those living or visiting close to the ocean, water activities were a bit more sophisticated.

Occasionally, water activities could get an avid fisherman into trouble when he stopped to toss in a line when he was supposed to be doing other things on behalf of his wife.

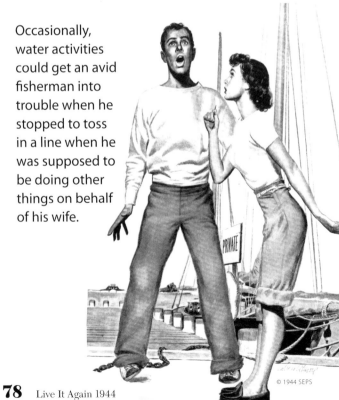

© 1944 SEPS

© 1944 SEPS

Everyday Life

On the farm

Hard times of World War II were not as difficult for farmers as they were for many in urban areas because farmers had learned to provide for their families and live in self-sufficiency through the hard times of the Great Depression. In some cases, farmers were requested to stay back and farm rather than go overseas, in order to provide for the nation's agricultural needs.

On farms where members of the family were drafted, others filled in. Children were asked to do major chores and assist with work that had been done by those who left. Gardening and preserving food was a way of life. Self-sufficiency also included providing one's own milk, butter and eggs.

Still, there was time for outings at the Grange Hall, parties at school or fellowship gatherings at the local rural church.

Families lived in multi-generational settings on many farms. Often, the presence of Grandma and Grandpa provided stability and encouragement to grandchildren in the absence of those serving in war.

"Anyone we know?"

Everyday Life

On the ranch

For the most part, life on the ranch was basically undisturbed in 1944. The government tried to leave as many farmers and ranchers in the country as possible, in order to continue fostering the nation's food supply. Ranch life was a cooperative of chores and efforts from everyone in the family, due to the large expanse of land that was covered and the amount of work to be covered in a day's time. Men and women alike were all part of the team.

A good horse provided friendship and relaxation from a hard day's work.

Men and women alike were involved in heavy work such as moving cattle and tending to livestock.

A break for some homemade coffee was a good way to plan out a day's work that would stretch over many miles of ranch land.

Everyday Life
Man's best friend

Puppies were cute, but their objects of play were sometimes misguided when they tore up ration stamps or important documents of the time. Still, they brought company to lonely children who missed their loved ones overseas.

When Pooch decided to raise a family, it made things interesting around the home. Children were assigned specific chores tending to the needs of the litter.

"Adds a convincing touch, doesn't it?"

"But, mother, he likes it that way!"

The innocence and candor of children provided amusement and a sense of normalcy to wartime America.

"Stinks, doesn't it?" *Mary Gibson*

"Didn't the characters seem a little flimsy to you?" *Rodney deSarro*

"Well, dear, what new words did Junior learn today?"

"Aren't you ashamed? You're the only unemployed kid in the block!"

Everyday Life

Back to school

Going back to school was always an exciting time, especially for those in rural areas who might not have seen certain friends since spring. The week before, school clothes were prepared, often sewn by moms and grandmas bent on saving money. School books were purchased, often in secondhand sales, or they were passed down from older siblings.

In homes where fathers had gone off to war, mothers were called upon to take on extra responsibilities and other family members all filled in. Sometimes, students, lonely for parents or relatives, would struggle with concentration in classes. However, teachers and coaches took on role model responsibilities to assist in keeping life as normal as possible.

REPRINTED WITH PERMISSION OF REVERE COPPER INC.

© 1944 SEPS

Some students, lonely for those gone to war, would struggle with daydreaming and becoming anxious over the safety of their loved ones.

REPRINTED WITH PERMISSION OF GENERAL MOTORS

Even the family pet took an interest in young boys as they did car repairs on their models.

The Metro Daily News

FINAL EDITION

OCTOBER 8, 1944

THE ADVENTURES OF OZZIE AND HARRIET DEBUTS
on CBS Radio in the United States.

Everyday Life

Junior engineers

A cover of "Saturday Evening Post" in December of 1944, depicted a young boy constructing a balsam airplane. Constructing model airplanes and cars was the rage of the day. Often when they broke, they were repaired as though a real automobile was being fixed.

Grass fields or even small airports were popular hangouts on Sunday afternoons when men and teenagers would gather to fly gasoline-powered model airplanes. Sometimes there would be shows or races.

As putting together models became more popular, young people developed large collections. Young and old got into the new hobby; often, fathers would sit beside their sons and put together famous ships, taking a considerable amount of time stringing the sails.

In addition, models became popular Christmas gifts, or special activities for such community organizations as Boys and Girls Club and Boy Scouts.

It didn't take long for the adults in the family to become intrigued by the construction of model planes. Sometimes, they were called upon to provide assistance for some of the more difficult projects.

The delicate work of engineering toy construction was often the most popular activity for youth on cold winter nights.

For older fellows, outside engineering projects required more time and thought. Some of them became successful scout projects.

Everyday Life

Soothing music

The concept of music therapy developed during World War I and II when musicians would visit hospitals of the wounded and play soothing music. Soon, community musicians of all types, amateur and professional, went to veteran hospitals around the country to play for thousands of veterans suffering from both physical and emotional wounds. The overall improvement of most patients was so remarkable that many hospitals began hiring musicians to perform for patients.

Neighborhood friends would also gather in the evenings in homes or on front lawns to enjoy their instruments and appreciate stress relief from the woes of the nation at war and the economic distress of the times.

On a professional level, it was soon discovered that the hospital musicians needed some prior training before entering the facility and so the demand grew for a college curriculum. As a result, the first music therapy degree in the world was founded at Michigan State University in 1944.

The joy of music brought soothing relief to a nation stressed and worried about their loved ones and the economy during World War II.

"This afternoon, in the absence of our regular conductor—"

FAMOUS BIRTHDAYS

Peter Tosh, October 19 Jamaican singer and musician

Ray Downs, October 24 American author and country music musician

Dennis Franz, October 28 American actor

Traveling to the concert hall on city buses was a challenge for many musicians.

"The Maestro doesn't appear to be in the mood tonight."

The Metro Daily News

FINAL EDITION

OCTOBER 21, 1944

AACHEN, THE FIRST GERMAN CITY TO FALL, IS CAPTURED BY AMERICAN TROOPS.

Top Hits of 1944

"Swinging On a Star"
Bing Crosby

"Straighten Up and Fly Right"
The Nat King Cole Trio

"Don't Fence Me In"
Bing Crosby and The Andrews Sisters

"Do Nothing Till You Hear From Me"
Duke Ellington

"I'll Be Seeing You"
Bing Crosby

"I Love You"
Bing Crosby

"I'm Making Believe"
Ella Fitzgerald and The Ink Spots

"Hamp's Boogie Woogie"
Lionel Hampton

"G.I. Jive"
Johnny Mercer With Paul Weston's Orchestra

"Solo Flight"
Benny Goodman

"Gee Baby, Ain't I Good to You"
The Nat King Cole Trio

"Main Stem"
Duke Ellington

Music & Radio

As the main source of in-home entertainment, the radio brought music, comedy, drama and news to an eager audience. In November 1944, half of the families in America tuned in to listen to election coverage when President Franklin D. Roosevelt defeated Thomas Dewey to win his fourth term. Radio time devoted to news rose to new levels in 1944, but music dominated much of the airwaves. As a result, stars like Bing Crosby saw stunning success. With hits like "I Love You," "Swinging on a Star" and "I'll Be Seeing You," Crosby's songs spent 20 weeks as the best-selling singles in retail stores.

Bing Crosby and The Andrews Sisters—Patty, LaVerne and Maxene—paired up to record several hits during 1944. They claimed the top spot on the song charts during the last two weeks of December with "Don't Fence Me In."

One of the best scat singers in the world, Ella Fitzgerald dazzled audiences with a voice spanning three octaves. Fitzgerald and The Ink Spots reached the top of the music charts in 1944 with "I'm Making Believe."

© CORBIS

"Good evening, friends," President Franklin D. Roosevelt's voice broadcast across the radio waves during one of his "fireside chats." In the heart of the "Golden Age of Radio," Roosevelt's weekly addresses often attracted more listeners than the most popular radio shows.

Edward R. Murrow brought the realities of the war to the airwaves and into the homes of the American people. Murrow flew along on multiple Allied bombing missions and vividly described the sights he witnessed.

Long and shoulder-length hairstyles were the fashion of the time.

Women of Intrigue

Most women, when dressed up, wore seamed stockings, pumps, hats, gloves and red lipstick. They often sought to fashion themselves after Hollywood stars pictured in movie posters. They wore solid colors, prints and plaid designs in order to appear confident and poised.

Hollywood personality figures often led the way for clothing trends of the day.

Women were not considered appropriately dressed unless they wore Sunday best garments to attend public social outings.

Solid gray and figured print dresses were both considered leaders in fashion for that special night out.

Cityscapes

Retail stores were located on the downtown square. People usually flocked to town on Saturdays with their list of items to be purchased at local dime stores and drug stores. Most downtown areas were enhanced by the town square, flanked by the American flag.

Neighborhood youth often rode their bikes to the corner meat market for a purchase from a list prepared by their mother. This usually included a friendly chat with the store owner as well.

Trains

America's work horse

Record setting volume in both passenger and freight service occurred between 1942 and 1944, due mainly to passenger trains being overloaded with large troop movements taking place to and from forts and staging areas in the country. Even though railroad companies tried to keep the public informed about times when there would be longer waits in stations, train travelers moved around in record volume.

One method of attempting to delay civilian travel was to run advertisements depicting images of fighting men returning home on trains.

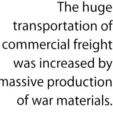

The huge transportation of commercial freight was increased by massive production of war materials.

The changeover from more primitive steam trains to large modern trains occurred quickly, especially with the demand of passenger service for troop movement across the country.

THE SATURDAY EVENING
POST

JUNE 3, 1944   10¢

© 1944 SEPS

The sight of an engineer
passing through a rural
area always invited
"open dialogue" with
local residents along the
way. The passing of large
numbers of commercial
trains through tranquil
rural countrysides
increased dramatically
between 1942 and 1944.

AIRPORT OF ACES
By CECIL CARNES

Can Americans and
Britons be Friends?
By BERTRAND RUSSELL

THE WEATHER
City and State—Rain.
Snow. Cyclone.
Storm in 1919 below.

VOLUME 67 — No. 151

The Metro Daily News

FINAL
EDITION

79 PAGES   FIVE CENTS

DECEMBER 16, 1944

GERMANY BEGINS THE
ARDENNES OFFENSIVE,
LATER KNOWN AS BATTLE
OF THE BULGE.

Large auto companies converted aluminum from usage for vehicles to planes and war weapons. Once Americans realized the need, the nation began to save and recycle weapon material.

PONTIAC

United States soldiers gained an upper hand in many battles once weapons made by recycling auto material began pouring onto the scene.

CHEVROLET ★ ALUMINUM FORGE PLANT

Automotive Industry Adapts

In 1944, the auto industry was contributing substantially to war and weapon needs. Aluminum was utilized in war construction and auto companies such as Cadillac were building war planes. The auto industry had no cars to sell, but they stayed in the public eye with advertisements showing their contributions to the war effort.

Although there was an initial layoff of auto workers in Detroit when the manufacturing of automobiles was stopped, the workforce bounced back as war manufacturing plants began to build and hire workers.

Planes flying over Europe reflected United States' automotive commitment to America's victory in the war.

Army officials plan new strategy, based on new equipment supplied by American manufacturers.

On the Home Front

Cautious optimism

As hints of optimism began to emerge from time to time, Americans, who had sacrificed and been stymied in lifestyle by worry and concern, began to relax just a bit. Rationing relaxed briefly in some areas; restraints were taken off of meat rationing, but then re-established later in the year. Even though there were still some tough times to go through, a sense of cautious hope began to enter the minds of Americans.

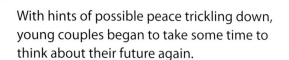

With hints of possible peace trickling down, young couples began to take some time to think about their future again.

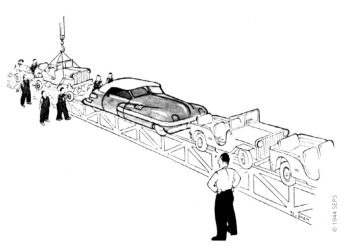

"Which one of you has been listening to peace rumors?"

"THERE'S A GREAT DAY COMIN'..."

Firestone
PRODUCING FOR WAR ✶✶ PREPARING FOR PEACE

TODAY, in all of its 58 factories throughout the world, Firestone is producing for war. Hundreds of different products made of rubber, metal and plastic are flowing forth in ever-increasing quantity from these busy Firestone plants — war materials that are saving American lives and helping to speed the day of victory. Under the impetus and inspiration of war-time emergency, Firestone has made many remarkable new discoveries and developed many startling new improvements in materials and machines, in processes and products. All of these technical advancements are now being concentrated on bringing the war to a quick and victorious conclusion.

VICTORY must come first, of course. But victory will be hollow indeed unless those on the home front plan now to help build that wonderful world of tomorrow for which millions of Americans are fighting. So Firestone is also preparing for peace. And after victory, when Firestone is again concentrating on peace-time products, its advantages in "know-how" will help provide work for its men and women now in service and enable Firestone to make and sell a wide variety of products which will set new standards of quality, durability, comfort and economy. So it is only natural that Firestone, while producing for war, is also preparing for peace.

PLASTIC LINERS FOR COMBAT HELMETS

AIRCRAFT AND AIRCRAFT PARTS

BARRAGE BALLOONS

BULLET-SEALING FUEL AND OIL CELLS

GUN TURRETS FOR TANKS

RAINCOATS, PONCHOS, WATER-REPELLENT FABRICS

INFLATABLE RAFTS, BOATS, PONTONS, BELTS AND VESTS

TIRES AND TUBES FOR ALL TYPES OF VEHICLES AND AIRCRAFT

BOFORS 40-MILLIMETER ANTI-AIRCRAFT GUNS

HOME, PORTABLE AND AUTOMOBILE RADIOS

WASHING MACHINES

REFRIGERATORS

GAS AND ELECTRIC RANGES

FOAMEX FOR MATTRESSES, FURNITURE, UPHOLSTERY AND SEATING

VELON FOR CLOTHING, HATS, SHOES, HOSIERY AND HUNDREDS OF OTHER USES

TIRES AND TUBES FOR ALL TYPES OF VEHICLES AND AIRCRAFT

CONTROL FOR FOUNDATION GARMENTS, SWIMMING SUITS AND MANY OTHER

BACK THE ATTACK—BUY WAR BONDS

Posters such as this one promoted by Firestone advocated a balanced sense of hope, but caution, in an attempt to promote a bit of encouragement and positive hope among Americans.

THE WEATHER

The Metro Daily News
FINAL EDITION

VOLUME 97 — No. 361

36 PAGES   FIVE CENTS

DECEMBER 26, 1944

THE GLASS MENAGERIE BY TENNESSEE WILLIAMS PREMIERES.

Voters lined up outside a polling station in Arlington, VA. An estimated 56 percent of eligible voters participated in the presidential election of 1944.

Elections of 1944

Few believed President Franklin D. Roosevelt would lose his office to Republican candidate Thomas E. Dewey in the 1944 election, and for good reason. Despite his ailing health and the fact that the war allowed Roosevelt little time to focus on his campaign, Roosevelt remained widely popular. When the polls closed on November 7, Roosevelt won 432 electoral votes to Dewey's 99. However, the popular vote was much closer than the electoral votes reflected, giving Roosevelt a narrower margin of victory compared to his other presidential races.

The incumbent president or the governor of New York? In the end, voters like these re-elected Franklin D. Roosevelt to a record fourth term. However, Roosevelt didn't complete his new term. Just five months after the election, Roosevelt's ailing health defeated him. He died April 12, 1945.

JOHN FALTER

Winter fun, especially in rural areas, was homemade, with young people cleaning off ponds and creeks to play hockey and go ice skating. In the country, scenes of bobsleds carrying goodies from the country store could still be seen. Winter was still enjoyed as a season, with people creating ways and reasons to be outdoors when possible.

Soldiers stopping on the street to take interest in a small child reflected the spirit of Christmas and patriotism in a very meaningful way.

Crowded train stations were filled with the Christmas spirit as friends and family members arriving on the train brought armloads of Christmas gifts for loved ones.

More *The Saturday Evening Post Covers*

The Saturday Evening Post covers were works of art, many illustrated by famous artists of the time, including Norman Rockwell. Most of the 1944 covers have been incorporated within the previous pages of this book; the few that were not are presented on the following pages for your enjoyment.

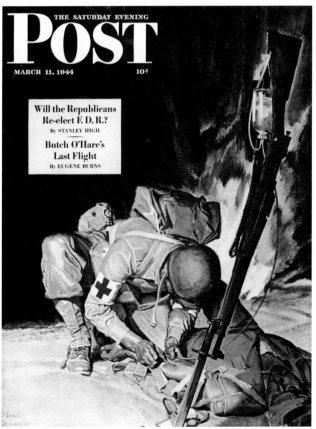

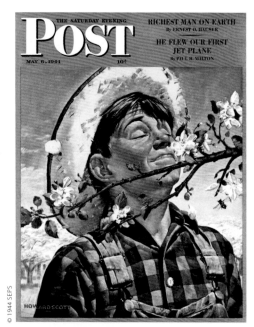

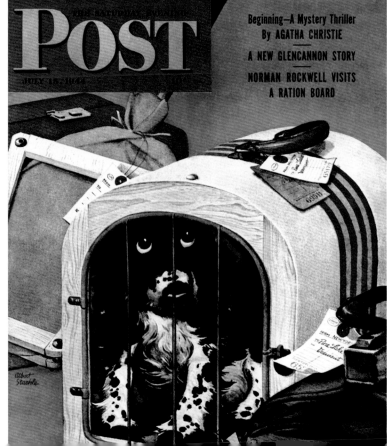

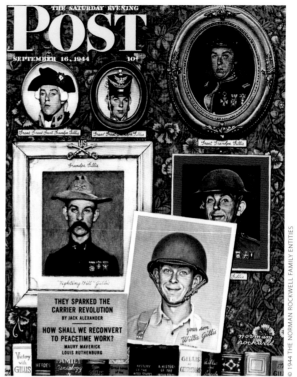

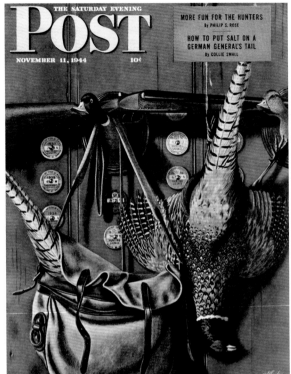

MORE FAMOUS BIRTHDAYS

January 1
Bob Minor, American actor and stunt performer

January 3
Chris von Saltza, American swimmer

January 6
Rolf M. Zinkernagel, Swiss immunologist, recipient of the Nobel Prize in Physiology or Medicine
Bonnie Franklin, American actress

January 9
Ian Hornak, American painter, draughtsman and sculptor

January 17
Françoise Hardy, French singer

January 18
Paul Keating, 24th Prime Minister of Australia

January 19
Shelley Fabares, American actress

January 25
Anita Pallenberg, Italian model and actress

January 27
Mairead Corrigan, Northern Irish activist, recipient of the Nobel Peace Prize
Nick Mason, English rock drummer and member of band Pink Floyd

January 28
John Tavener, British composer
Susan Howard, American actress

February 2
Geoffrey Hughes, British actor

February 3
Trisha Noble, Australian singer and actress

February 5
Al Kooper, American rock musician and member of band Blood, Sweat & Tears

February 11
Michael G. Oxley, American politician

February 12
Moe Bandy, Country music singer

February 13
Jerry Springer, English-born American television host
Stockard Channing, American actress

February 14
Alan Parker, English-born film director, actor and writer

February 16
Richard Ford, American writer

February 17
Karl Jenkins, Welsh composer

February 20
Willem van Hanegem, Dutch soccer player and coach

February 22
Jonathan Demme, American film director, producer and writer
Tom Okker, Dutch tennis player

February 23
Johnny Winter, American rock musician

February 27
Ken Grimwood, American writer

February 28
Sepp Maier, German soccer player

March 1
John Breaux, U.S. Senator from Louisiana

March 2
Uschi Glas, German actress

March 4
Harvey Postlethwaite, British engineer and race car designer
Bobby Womack, American singer and songwriter

March 5
Peter Brandes, Danish artist

March 6
Kiri Te Kanawa, New Zealand soprano

Mary Wilson, American singer and member of vocal group The Supremes

March 8
Buzz Hargrove, Canadian labor leader

March 11
Don Maclean, British comedian

March 17
John Sebastian, American singer and songwriter and member of vocal group The Lovin' Spoonful

March 19
Sirhan Sirhan, Palestinian assassin of Robert F. Kennedy

March 21
Hilary Minster, British actor

March 24
R. Lee Ermey, U.S. Marine and actor

March 28
Rick Barry, American basketball player

April 6
Felicity Palmer, English soprano

April 7
Gerhard Schröder, former Chancellor of Germany

April 8
Odd Nerdrum, Norwegian painter
Jimmy Walker, American professional basketball player

April 13
Jack Casady, American rock musician and member of band Jefferson Airplane

April 19
James Heckman, American economist, Nobel Prize laureate

April 22
Steve Fossett, American aviator, sailor and millionaire adventurer

April 27
Michael Fish, British TV weatherman

April 30
Jill Clayburgh, American actress

Live It Again 1944

PROJECT EDITOR	Richard Stenhouse
ASSISTANT EDITOR	Erika Mann
ART DIRECTOR	Brad Snow
COPYWRITER	Jim Langham
MANAGING EDITOR	Barb Sprunger
EDITORIAL ASSISTANTS	Stephanie Smith, Jennifer Sprunger
PRODUCTION ARTIST SUPERVISOR	Erin Augsburger
PRODUCTION ARTISTS	Erin Augsburger, Nicole Gage, Edith Teegarden
COPY EDITOR	Amanda Scheerer
PHOTOGRAPHY SUPERVISOR	Tammy Christian
NOSTALGIA EDITOR	Ken Tate
COPY SUPERVISOR	Michelle Beck
EDITORIAL DIRECTOR	Jeanne Stauffer
PUBLISHING SERVICES DIRECTOR	Brenda Gallmeyer

Printed in China
First Printing: 2010
Library of Congress Number: 2009904231
ISBN: 978-1-59635-277-3

Customer Service
LiveItAgain.com
(800) 829-5865

1 2 3 4 5 6 7 8 9